My Daughter Is An Astronaut.

Claudia Valdés

ENGLISH TRANSLATION: ©LIDICE MEGLA

EDITORIAL LUNETRA

MY DAUGHTER IS AN ASTRONAUT

To, For, By, According to, About, After Lucia...
And for anyone who might need such a book.

"God could not be everywhere, and therefore he made the mothers."

Puck of Pook's Hill
RUDYARD KIPLING

DON'T GIVE UP

This book was written with a lot of heart by a mother with the strength, determination, and dedication to investigate everything within her reach and beyond to improve her daughter's life.

The work Claudia has done for Lucia is moving and exemplary. It has broken all diagnostics: some doctors said Lucia would never walk. Others that she wouldn't talk either. Yet she has been jumping all those barriers, like a rider on the back of a spirited steed, almost winged, and that winged steed is her mother, Claudia.

All that Claudia has done – what she has lived, experienced, and learned on this long road – she has wanted to pour into these pages as a guide, an encouragement, a consolation for other mothers and fathers who have been overwhelmed by the arrival of an atypical child as if their world were falling apart.

And Claudia, in this book, tells them that this is not the case. We want to share what that experienced and compassionate neurologist said to us that afternoon with all parents in the same situation. He told us, "It's up to Lucia, and only Lucia can show us what she will do in life."

In a way, that's the message of this book.

We don't know the limits; We only know from experience that true miracles can be worked with much work, passion, and hope.

Life is a mystery, and the human brain is as big a mystery as life. The same specialists confess that, in some respects, they do not know everything. Atypical children, even if they seem limited, are capable of achievements that would seem impossible. Still, these can be changed with the hard therapeutic work, support, and understanding of a collaborative family that is always determined to turn difficulties into challenges.

It's not an easy road, but nothing worthwhile in the world has been easy. Sometimes, you cry, sometimes you get frustrated, and sometimes the hill seems too steep, but there are also moments of immense joy. A joy so great that parents of neurotypical children will never be able to experience. They never saw it as difficult, distant, almost impossible. And then, when the goal is achieved, it is as happy as the accomplishment of a miracle.

This is a book to tell many parents: don't give up, don't get tired, don't think it's impossible, and above all, remember that it's not for you. It's for your child. And you'll see how much it's worth.

I have witnessed that miracle that Claudia, with enormous enthusiasm and tenacity, and of course, with the help of many people, has been achieving. And it keeps succeeding. Because the road is endless, and what Lucia will be, only Lucia will tell us.

Enjoy this book and have faith!

ALEXIS VALDÉS
(Lucia's Dad)

PREFACE

How much does a ticket to the moon cost?

To your Moon? I asked myself, looking into those eyes as dark as the cats that roam my neighborhood.

If I could get that ticket and travel there with her, maybe I'd understand everything faster.

What would that Moon of yours be like? What size? What color? Can you skip rope there? I wondered what time it usually takes for her to return to reality.

I have an astronaut daughter, and I still don't know anything about the planets she visits.

Yes, my daughter travels to the cosmos with her gaze, and she stays there for a few seconds that are eternal for me, and that's why I invent all kinds of big gestures and clicks to bring her back to this world because the world I know is the "normal" one.

But what if her world is far more magical and interesting than mine?

Why deprive her of flying to the moon? And what's more, without paying for a ticket?

From the moment she began to leave her gaze fixed nowhere, I understood that I would get to know the cosmos with her. It would not be easy, but thanks to having her, I would also fly out of this world and go with her to her world.

The world of the autism spectrum.

CLAUDIA VALDÉS,
Mother of an astronaut.

"Autism is a syndrome that is characterized by several developmental deficits, deficits in verbal and nonverbal communication; deficits in social interaction, repetitive restrictive behaviors, and sensory disturbances."

DR. EMME CORRALES REYES

MD. NEUROLOGIST

MY BEST TEACHER

I think I'm a bit of a witch, not like the ones who make spells and magic potions and scare children with cliché laughter, but a little witch who can sense things.

I always felt that my path as a mom wouldn't exactly be the most comfortable. Something made me think that the day I had a daughter (because I always knew it would be a girl), my little girl would be "different."

I spent my pregnancy reading books that were supposed to prepare me to be a mom. HA! No manual serves as a better guide for a mother or father than their child; that's why I am writing this book because my daughter has been my best teacher and the truth? It would have been beneficial for me then to read something like this, which would have helped me understand, process, and look for solutions to the "news."

CHAPTER I

THE EXPLOSION OF THE BABY BOTTLE

Lucía was born with a "small pool" on her head, like a puddle the size of a penny. It's called Aplasia Cutis Congenita (if you're like me you're going to run and look it up on the internet, don't do it, later I'll explain in detail why) ... It's something harmless if it's small like hers. Still, it will leave a little mark forever, where no hair will ever grow again (She has a lot of hair anyway.)

During the first days after her birth, we cleaned it every two hours with an ointment that I imagined was magical, and I visualized that with each smear, it would heal completely... And so, it did. It healed in the shape of an almost perfect heart as if a painter elf had drawn it and, as her hair grew, the mark was no longer visible, although now and then I still make my way through a lot of hair to check it and make sure that everything is fine.

I treated her as if she were made of glass. She was so small and fragile (like any newborn baby) that everything around her, any noise, the light, the dust, life itself scared me.

I had a hard time breastfeeding her, partly because it was something new to me. I was hurting and tired, and I also suffered a mild postpartum depression, which I understood and accepted later. I questioned the mixture of feelings within me. It was as if I had put a lot of sensations in a bottle and stirred them before drinking, as they recommend on juice labels.

I looked at Lucia, and all the happiness and fears I had never experienced were contained in her dark eyes, but

19

in her eyes was also the cure to my fears. And Lucia came to this world with certainty in her eyes.

"You grew up with formula milk and a friend's breast milk, and look how well you turned up," my mom told me on the terrible day of the bottle explosion.

That afternoon, I was very stressed and sad and started using those automatic breast pumps that make a noise between funny and worrying. With a lot of work, I managed to fill half a bottle, but it is possible that I did not close it tightly because, after a few seconds, the lid flew out as if, instead of milk, I had poured gunpowder on it, and the bottle was empty, after all that work to extract some... That day, I ran out of what little milk I had.

So, we turned to formula, the delicacy that helped me feed my daughter, and in each feeding, I was reminded that I had not been able to do my job, that in that test of "being a mother," I had failed her, but I've never said it, until now.

Myth or Reality, Breastfeeding? Knowing that your baby is nourishing itself directly from you is something unique that makes every mother feel very proud. It is also one of the first pieces of advice everyone gives you, "as soon as you give birth, try to give her milk from your breast for as long as possible."

I had never told anyone about this until now, but when I saw that I couldn't do it, I felt a profound sadness. I went out into the backyard and found a blind spot by the fence between the boundary of our house and the neighbors, and looking and feeling messy and outdated,

I let it all out; I cried, still not understanding this task appointed to us by mother nature when she created us.

"I have already failed at the basics, and this is just the beginning," I told myself that day, also the last day I blamed myself for anything related to my daughter.

The truth is that many mothers can breastfeed, and many others cannot, and this does not put one or the other on a poster of the best or the worst mother of the month. Formula, as my mother told me, also nourishes, and here I am to prove it with all the others raised with milk other than breast milk. So, if you couldn't breastfeed long enough, or none at all, erase all guilt from your mind, and, if you can, apply it to everything else you feel guilty about in your entire life.

The first months passed between a deep cloudiness of tiredness, sleepiness, dark circles, sleeplessness, anguish, happiness, uncertainty, fears, and tears (hers and mine) ... It's so weird to be a mom.

My daughter was growing at the normal healthy standard rate. Her weight and eating seemed to be within the normal and the established. Then, at six months old, my mom and I realized something was not in line with what was "normal and established." There were slight indications because it is too early to think about any diagnosis at that age, but a mother's instinct NEVER fails. Lucía did not have the strength required to stand up, which is the most common thing at six months since babies can already be held below the shoulders and support themselves on their legs. Lucia did not try to crawl either. Perhaps other parents would have waited, but I decided to start looking for the reason causing that delay, especially in the motor area.

And this is where this book begins.

THE TINY BOX OF INFORMATION

Imagine that you have in front of you an apparently small box of matches in your favorite color. I say apparently because, in reality, this box is only as big as your ability to deal with situations over which you have no control. So, if we put our minds to it, this box could be huge. When you open it, it has no limits of space to quantify all that fits inside it. This box is my gift to you. In it, you can fit every bit of valuable information that you can find in this book or any other. I will call this information "matches of light," they will help you create the orange flame with which you will light your way as a mother of an autistic child.

As everything is symbolic, whenever I see here that I have a match for you to light, I will let you know so that you can scratch it with a marker to form the map that best suits you to achieve the incalculable progress of your little astronaut.

CHAPTER II

EVERY CHILD IS DIFFERENT.

The phrase I've heard the most in the last four years is "EVERY CHILD IS DIFFERENT." I had listened to it so much that I was about to get it tattooed. Ultimately, I chose a different phrase that defined my path: "One Day At a Time." I carry it on my arm. On the other hand, I got a tattoo: Lucia.

The first advice I heard was always related to not comparing one child to another, which I did a lot. I don't want to deceive you or paint in a rosy color what was gray at times.

As a new mother, the first thing I did was to start comparing my daughter with other girls of similar ages, and it was the most logical thing to do if that's what doctors rely on to determine when something is "out of the ordinary," right? Isn't it the comparison with the rest of the children going to a "logical step" of development that determines the level of progress our children have? The answer is Yes, but that point of comparison should be used by professionals and, in any case, as a guide to determine our children's deficiencies to offer them the combination of therapies and treatments they need to move forward.

When I realized that I was making a huge mistake by putting my daughter under the bar of other children, I began to see everything differently. This is something that every parent must understand in depth, and with conviction and implementation, it would perhaps be the first match I would put in the box.

It took me a long time to understand that the comparison of my daughter's developmental process with that of other children only created a block of emotions in my head, and this acted as an impediment to looking for solutions, and this only made me sad, so I decided to stop looking for what other children were doing to start finding everything my daughter could do. And believe me, I was surprised. Every day, I am more and more surprised.

That's how I started organizing all of her symptoms so that I could better explain to the doctors why I thought my daughter needed an in-depth study. And here's another match for your information box. Write down on a piece of paper everything that worries you, everything that you feel is not right with your son or daughter. We mothers are intuitive; thus, as parents, we know what our children need.

With all my observations, plus those of my mother, my mother-in-law, Alexis, Lucia's father, and some things I heard or read here or there, I went to see the pediatrician. I told him all my doubts, especially that the most disturbing thing was that Lucía could not support her feet nicely and did not have the physical strength to support her body. I also told him about the slowness of her natural rhythm; everything was calm and peaceful. Lucía has constantly reminded me of peace.

Another detail that caught my attention was her lack of effort to speak and repeat words she heard. With all that and the luck of having the best pediatrician I could choose for my daughter, we began investigating. I will tell you about that process, but first, I want to leave you another magic match for the box where you collect information. It is imperative to find the best doctors for our children. The primary doctor or pediatrician will be essential throughout their childhood, especially if a boy or girl requires more attention than others. They will refer the case to specialists who will find and work on our children's difficulties later.

Doctors can become great allies in this process, so look carefully when choosing the one you will entrust your little one with. On the recommendation of a great friend, I was lucky to find one of the best pediatricians in Miami, where we live. His name is Octavio Vasconcello, and I will leave his reference at the end of the book with that of other doctors who have made this path easier. So, if you need them, do not hesitate to use them.

CHAPTER III

THE WORST DAY OF MY LIFE.

"Give me one reason not to die of fear and pain right here, right now, when my child looks so sick," I said a thousand times to God as I drove speeding to the hospital on the worst day of my life. Lucia was convulsing, and I didn't understand anything.

She was six months old. It all started with a silly fever of 37.3 degrees. She had a little flu, but it wasn't as serious as to be scared, as she was perfect, playing with my mom. Then, out of the blue, in an instant, her eyes were lost and unresponsive, like two distant stars. Her mouth opened, and she wouldn't react to anything. It all happened in a matter of seconds. My mom screamed, calling out for me, "Clau, the baby, the baby!" I took the baby and ran without any idea of what was wrong with her. Somehow, the switch in my brain went on automatically, and like a robot, I reacted. Alexis called 911, but I didn't have the patience to wait for help to arrive, so in less than 10 seconds, we were in the car, my mom with Lucia in the back, and Alexis next to me while I drove for dear live to the nearest hospital.

I want to describe the journey from our home to the hospital with words, but I can't find them. We still don't know how I got to the emergency room in nine minutes. I ran through all the red lights on the way there. I still don't understand how the police didn't stop us.

I remember my mom saying from behind, "Lucia, Lucia, react," while Alexis tried to calm me down, but I could only hear them from far away as if they were speaking to me from another dimension. Everything was surreal, and I drove like an automaton with only one goal: to get there as soon as possible and save my daughter from something I didn't even know what it was yet.

When we arrived at the emergency room, I parked the car in front of the front door, got out still in robot mode, and snatched it from my mom's arms. I ran in, opening all the doors, shouting, "Save my daughter! Save my daughter!" The doctors on duty came out very soon, picked her up, and said she was convulsing; that is, she was convulsing for 10 minutes or so, which is how long it took me to get there.

I ran with them into the living room, where they took off her clothes, gave her an injection, and stabilized her instantly. I exited my body for a few minutes and watched that scene from above. I saw myself stronger and more confident, standing next to my daughter, like any other doctor, my mother very nervous, screaming, and Alexis beside me, serene but undoubtedly scared to death as well. I didn't recognize myself; it wasn't me who was there. It was another woman, a brave and static woman. I didn't blink, I didn't move; I was just there like a rock, waiting for my daughter to react, to make eye contact with me. I didn't cry, I didn't complain, I didn't say a word until she looked at me with those eyes and the gaze that you know when your child is looking at you, their mother. And that's when I knew that she was okay, that she was the same Lucia as always.

Then I returned to my body and had the strength to say thank you to the doctors. I thanked them so much that they almost had to inject me to get me out of shock. No other word came out of my mouth other than Thank you. Thank you for saving my daughter; THANK YOU. I remember my mom's look as if she didn't recognize me. I also think she never expected to see her daughter with such grit in the most distressing moment of her life. I think she was very proud of me.

This event added one more pebble to the backpack with which Lucia came into the world, something more to investigate... Why did that seizure happen?

This question would be answered a year later.

That day, we stayed in the hospital. Lucía had to be admitted for tests and to rule out if the seizure caused any brain damage. It was the first time after giving birth that we slept together in a hospital room, and I wish it had been the last.

I didn't leave her all night; I sat next to her bed, looking at her and begging St. Lazarus that everything would be okay from then on. She behaved so well. The innocence of small children in moments like this is so favorable because they don't know what's going on, they don't understand what doctors are, they forget everything very quickly, the punctures, the nurses coming in every 15 minutes to check if everything was okay. That children of that age soon erase from their minds... We adults, their parents, don't.

We stayed in the hospital for two nights, and that's a weird feeling because nobody wants to be in a hospital, but at the same time, I felt protected there. I remember that the second night, when Lucía was already asleep, I went out to the hallway to stretch my legs without losing sight of her. Although my mom and I were both staying to watch Lucia (but I hope I'm not confusing this stay with the other time we were in the hospital, too...) Anyway, I went out to the hallway, and in the next room, I heard a mother crying desperately loudly. I think she had been given bad news about her son, and at that very moment, I had, perhaps, the most selfish thought of my life, but at the same time, it helped me feel a little better.

At first, I felt deeply for that mother. I haven't told you, but I'm an HSP[1] person (I'll talk about that later), and I can experience the pain of others, but that day, I found something that would make me feel so much better for everything I would face in the future. And here comes another little match, a little selfish, but maybe it will also make you, who read me, feel better.

There's always someone going through something worse, so if we focus on the fact that compared to other people, we're noticeably better off, we can feel some relief. At least, that's how I felt when I returned to the room where Lucia was sleeping. I looked at her and said to myself, "You're healthy, my daughter. Tomorrow, we're leaving here; some parents aren't that lucky."

The next day, we were given the results of the tests, and to our happiness, everything looked fine. It was time to go home.

---

[1] Highly Sensitive Person

CHAPTER IV

THE TESTS

After the convulsion incident, I developed a constant state of alarm. I was attentive to every movement of her eyes, and I was nervous, even more so when you don't know what exactly produced them. It is inevitable to live in fear that it will happen again. Luckily, it took many months for that distressing episode to repeat itself.

I had a lot of other things to focus on in Lucia regarding her development, so we began a long and tedious process of searching, trying in each exam to find everything that could be an alarm, an aspect to work on.

Around seven months old, she looked like a real astronaut for a while as she had to wear a head molding cap, a kind of helmet used by children who have their heads a little flat behind or in a specific area. Lucia's was not so remarkable, but the months she wore it helped her a lot to better mold the shape of her little head. I confess that I didn't put it on enough. I could see she was uncomfortable in it. I noticed she sweated profusely, and she felt like a prisoner in it, and this produced in me an incredible pain. Any thought was an excuse for me to take it off her for a while, and these little whiles turned into hours. Maybe she could wear it more often and for longer periods, but I'm not going to blame myself for that. In the end, she wore it for about six months, and we received a very cool diploma, her first diploma, which said that she had satisfactorily graduated from the use of the helmet. I breathed a sigh of relief because that little helmet, I think, it bothered me more than it did her.

Since I've been a mom, I've come to understand the meaning of mimicry. I have come to feel the same pains and feelings as my daughter. I have tried so hard and long to understand her discomforts and concerns that I ended up experiencing them, too. So, during those six months, I also wore the little helmet on my head.

Going out with a baby is directly proportional to people looking at you. Young children, especially, cause a lot of attention as they are very tender, and almost everyone likes to look at them or offer a compliment or kind word about them, especially when this child has something visible going on, something physical, something remarkable, like a helmet. The first days, everyone asked why the girl had to use it, and always, those who didn't know about it associated it with bigger problems than a simple deformation of the head, nothing serious, then you have to explain what it is and what it is used for. The first few times, I found myself giving thousands of explanations so that people would understand the reason why Lulu used it. Then I realized that it was not necessary to take all that time because really the reason was very simple and was summarized in a single sentence, "because she needs it," and that's it.

Explanations make us hostage to situations, and we can get entangled around something that is very simple. Of course, we all want our children to be within the "standard perfection" of society, and from that perfection comes everything that is not common: a wheelchair, crutches, listening devices, leg devices, head-shaping caps, etc., which are not commonly found around, and when they are, they arouse curiosity, and that curiosity of people who do not belong to our family circle, generates, consciously or unconsciously, a certain stress on us.

People should refrain from asking so many futile questions when they see a mother with a "different" child: "Oh, but what does she have?"... "And what's wrong with her?"... "Still not talking?... "When does she plan to walk? All these inopportune questions put us in a very uncomfortable situation, even if we don't want to. We can't control external opinions, but what we can control is not to allow ourselves to be affected in any way by the opinions of others. And this is a topic that I'll talk about in a whole chapter later on.

We continue with the tests.

By now, we have doctorates in analysis, tests, and specialists at home, as we take Lucía to so many doctors.

As I mentioned at the beginning, one of the things that worried me the most was that she still couldn't walk, and she was very hypotonic. Hypotonia refers to a decrease in muscle tone. This condition causes a child to be straighter and without interacting. It can be improved with therapies until it is completely eradicated, as with Lucia. We took her to an American orthopedist, and here comes a story that brings to light one of the most important matches in this book.

Doctors know a lot about general statistics; in fact, they base their diagnosis on a series of symptoms that, by similarity, characterize a disease or ailment. I have a lot of respect for the work of doctors, and I am grateful that most of the ones that have passed through my life, and my daughter's, have been wonderful. It is also important that we give credit to the little inner doctor that we mothers always have on call. And it's not about contradicting the diagnoses, not at all, but it is about being able to look beyond, to look for the Yes to a No, and here is a very clear example of this.

We arrived at the Orthopedics office after waiting quite a bit for an appointment. Alexis, Lucía, and I were expectant, especially for him to tell us about solutions to what we already knew our daughter had. Knock Knees (or Genu Valgum) occurs when a child stands up and their knees touch, but their ankles are separated. "X-shaped legs" usually pass as a normal part of growth and development. This time, it is always a little scary as doctors will usually tell you it corrects itself, but I wanted to know if wearing braces on her feet would help her more. I thought that was what kept Lucia from walking.

The doctor's response—who examined Lucía only for a few minutes as if she were a class object of no importance—was that Lucía wasn't going to walk, that he didn't see it possible.

We were silent for a little while, and then we asked him again. We wanted to know if we were understanding him correctly, and he said what he said: "I don't think she can walk." Well, he said it in English: "I don't think she is going to be able to walk."

When you receive news like this, you have two options: cry out, get depressed, think it's the end of the world, or get up, say 'thank you for your time' and walk out resolved to exhaust every possible way without getting tired and show yourself and your daughter that diagnoses are not definitive.

I think it's obvious which way we are going.

Of course, it's also valid to experience the first option, crying, worrying, yelling, Hey! After all, it's normal to feel afraid of the unknown; crying doesn't make you any less strong or less capable. Crying relieves you, and also clarifies your ideas. The real strength lies in, even with those tears soaking your face, having the courage to stand and face all and every obstacle with your daughter by the hand, and like the robot character, Voltus V, make her literally fly!

Chapter V

"Robot Mom"

I am a robot mom. I truly see myself as such, and that's also a useful way of survival. I have always thought that anything that brings strength of spirit and peace of mind should be welcomed into our lives. A mom comes with these ingredients by default, but sometimes, we need so much more than what Mother Nature gives us.

We could call everything that arms us with courage Faith; that powerful word contains the strength to move mountains. So, with faith, strength of spirit, and peace of mind ahead of us, and many fears behind us, we decided not to let into our minds what that doctor told us.

Lucía was already nine months old. She sat perfectly and could stay seated for a long time, but she still didn't support her legs; she didn't even try, and she didn't crawl at all.

My pediatrician, Octavio Vasconcello, recommended starting with physical therapies to achieve muscle mass. That's how I found the center that welcomed my daughter and so many other children I know with immense love and even greater knowledge, and here is another match for you to light.

The world of therapies was unknown to me. When Lucía started, she was still a baby, and we had no idea about future diagnoses. I was only worried that she wasn't walking for her age group and that she would not walk, so perhaps, like many other mothers at the beginning, I arrived with a bit of resistance to the center that I am now going to talk about.

Why resistance? I guess because we all want our kids to follow the natural path everyone else follows, and most kids, to my knowledge, didn't go to therapy. I didn't know how wrong I was with that kind of thought!

That's why this little piece here is a little match. Because I want to try and help remove the fear many parents feel when they hear the word "therapy."

Due to my lack of knowledge, I came to associate my daughter going to therapy with labels that society could put on her. This absurd thought only lasted one day: the day I arrived at Florida Kids Therapy, the center that introduced me to this new world and made me fall in love entirely with it. I've been enormously lucky, and above all, I've let myself be guided by people who know.

When I arrived at this magical place (because they do pure magic there), I understood not only that therapies would be the starting point of any progress for my daughter but also that there were many children, many with and without diagnoses, who benefited from them.

There are three fundamental therapies provided at these centers: Physical Therapy, Speech Therapy, and Occupational Therapy.

For those who are not familiar, I will tell you a little about what each one is about.

Physical therapy can help children with motor skill delays or limited mobility. Speech Therapy is an intervention with the goal of improving a child's ability to understand and express language. A medical professional, called a speech-language pathologist, performs the therapy. These pathologists[2] evaluate, diagnose, treat, and help prevent speech, language, and communication disorders. Occupational Therapy helps children with disabilities or lack physical, sensory, or cognitive skills to carry out everyday tasks such as eating, putting on socks and shoes, focusing on learning, writing, or playing with toys or other children.

This is, broadly speaking, a very basic description of the therapies to which I owe much of my daughter's incredible progress. So, store it in the little box as a very important match.

I remember that when I arrived at the center, I was given a tour of the facilities to see how they worked with the children, the different therapy rooms, and how they were used. That was the first time I saw a case of severe autism. In one of the classrooms, decorated with a lot of love and bright colors, there was a child sitting with his back on a wall lined with the alphabet. A therapist in a blue uniform with a very sweet speech was with him; she frequently redirected the boy's attention. He made repetitive movements and strongly moved his head back and forth. He was very restless, and out of nowhere, he started screaming and hurting himself; it all happened very fast, and I didn't have time to assimilate what I was seeing. I hurried to another room, and from there, I could hear his therapist calming him down until the screaming stopped. I'm not going to

---

[2] Speech-language pathologist (SLP).

deny it: I was very impressed and automatically thought of this boy's mom. What would her life be like at home? How did she react when he got like that? I had no answers, and at the same time, I felt a great relief to know that there was a place, or rather, several places, with professionals trained to help these children and, more importantly, also to teach parents how to understand and handle them best.

Up to this point, autism had no relation to my life. I came to this center to encourage my daughter, through therapies, to advance in several physical and social issues that she had not yet been able to explore; therefore, seeing from my own eyes this first contact with autistic children, all so different, was awakening my curiosity to know more.

There is so much that we don't know about, right? So many diagnoses that we know of their existence by hearsay, but we never bother to investigate further. It is curious how life makes us live through them to know them truly.

When I left the center, I started to investigate a little more, to ask here and there, and with all the information, I found how positive therapies are for children with any delay or difficulty, whether or not they have a diagnosis, I came to the conclusion that, if we consistently combined these three therapies and started as soon as possible, Lucía would go a long way in all aspects, so that's what I did.

At the age of nine months, Lucía began to receive these three types of therapies on a regular basis, which have been fundamental to her development.

My little flower continued to grow and sprout, adorning my garden. The therapies made a noticeable difference, especially the physical one, which had been our main concern until then. Sometimes, the therapists would come to our house, and sometimes, we would take her to the center.

They did all kinds of exercises, with big and small balls and ropes, always motivating her to try to reach the toys in front of her and stimulating her senses and motor skills. The living room of our house looked like a professional gym.

Lucia's tendency has always been towards the slow. She has set her own rhythm to do things calmly; she is the opposite of restlessness and nervousness, always slow, and so it was like this with the therapy. At first, she cried. Of course, no one likes to be forced to make physical exertion. I remember that her father and I would hide behind the door so as not to be seen by her and so that she would pay full attention to the therapist. Still, sometimes she cried so much that I, in an irrepressible impulse of a protective mother, would open the door and ask the therapist to stop. I did it a lot. I felt an immediate need to help her; she was so small that I couldn't help feeling that, in some way, she was forced to do those exercises that seemed tremendous to me but that, in truth, were common and also very necessary to help her muscles become strong.

Eventually, I stopped interrupting the sessions. I understood that therapy time is sacred and that she should and must understand the power of effort to achieve something, and if just for crying I was going to be stopping the exercises every five minutes, then I was attacking her evolution (life is much stronger than a therapy session, won't I know it...) So, I let the professionals do their job, and, in the process, I also learned their techniques and then put them into practice.

Occupational therapies helped a lot; everything was prepared to activate her senses and develop her fine and gross motor skills, and above all, in working with textures, we realized that Lucía tended to reject many types of textures. Fluffy things produced a sort of aversion on her, and sand, grains of rice, or wet balls filled with water made her gag. Those were also the first indications that supported my suspicion to listen to the voice of "there's something else here."

I've always been a bit of a reading worm. I really like to do research and being in contact with the therapy center, which allowed me to observe children with different stereotypes associated with autism, and this was definitely one of them, the sensory part was like the red-light bulb that went on to tell me that something needed to be checked.

In speech therapies at that time, we didn't make much progress. Lucia's world was like in a silent comedy movie... Not a word.

Chapter VI

Lucia, My Silent Film:

A chapter about silence and all the noise it usually comes with.

It is every mother's dream to hear that tender little voice saying the magic word capable of melting the thickest iron: "Mama." I still don't know the spell it produces or if it makes us feel more important to be called "mom" than to be called a doctor or a graduate because Mom is like a title of nobility, like standing on a carpet and flying to your child's feet and receiving his or her voice with an open heart.

Anything goes to make this miracle happen, something that may be very natural for most children, but for some, it is tough and, for others, almost impossible.

Lucia was nonverbal until she was three years old. I learned to communicate with her through the huge, open window of her eyes, by the gestures of her hands, and by the tenacity with which she led us to the toy or food she wanted at that moment. I hadn't given importance to the power of pointing until she showed it to me. There are so many ways to communicate besides voice that I learned how to guess her thoughts.

I had a lot of uncertainty, I'm not going to deny it, and fear that it would be like this forever, but my faith and the perseverance that we poured into speech therapies and giving her a lot of stimuli was stronger. Lucía has been the real key to her entire achievement. She's stubborn and goes all the way when she wants to achieve something, just like me. Many parents told me, "Hey, don't worry, mine was the same, and he/she spoke at the age of four, and now he/she doesn't shut up." Others told me their children didn't speak anything until the age of six, and now, they speak three languages and that sometimes, they (the parents) even want to say, "Oh, shut up for a while." I prayed to God and all the saints for the same thing to happen to me. I wanted to be able to say, "Oh Lucia, shut up, you are making me dizzy from so much talking," as I used to say to my brother, who did not stop talking when he was little, but at that moment, that possibility felt very far away. I didn't know what her voice was like. We talked to her, and she didn't answer a word. We lived at home in the purest and most innocent silence, like in a silent era film, subtitled only by the language of her gestures and her little fingers, by her eyes and my intuition, full of laughter too, because Lucía loves to laugh. Her laughter was the noise that broke all muteness; her laughter was the battery needed to charge the flashlight to my strength to light up the way for me to continue looking for solutions to hear her call me Mom.

I confess that I often cried with the same silence that she gave me. I cried, wondering where she was going with her lost eyes, which sometimes seemed to be flying over the earth. I cried with that deep pain that uncertainty generates, and because I was afraid of not fulfilling that desire, the desire to hear her call me MOM.

Her first word was Dad, and it was very curious because her "Dad" had two meanings: her father and everything else. She differentiated it by the voice's cadence, depending on what she was referring to, such was the intonation she gave it! Dad (for Alexis, her father) was *papáaaa "Papa," the word babies usually call the word food in Spanish was shorter and more concise,* and when she referred to me, she also said papa, but don't ask me how I knew she was referring to me. The

56

awakening of her words was very slow, and her voice, the most beautiful I have ever heard in my life.

Lucia

Scan to Listen

Lucia's voice giving me a profound lesson.

Drawing of Lucia

Chapter VII

Making a Living

I mentioned that Lucia's first months of therapy were in our home.

It was very comfortable for us, too, because we could hear and, somehow, see and learn from all the therapists. Lulu was advancing at her own pace; every day, we noticed that she was interacting more with us, and she was creating a very positive chemistry with her therapists. Until the pandemic hit, that experience that for the first time came with the uncertainty we would all equally experience later on, and from which I also drew several lessons applicable if we draw a parallel with whatever it is that we are experiencing and has us deeply dismayed. Now, I'm going to explain why.

At the most critical moment of the Covid 19 pandemic, when the lockdown was ordered in the United States, we all changed the life plans to which our routine was adapted. Like any resounding change, it generated new programming in our minds and in our capacity for resilience. When I say everyone, I don't mean my whole family, but all human beings.

Lucía's father, Alexis, was on the air in one of the highest-rated late-night shows on Miami television. I was the general producer and also an actress in the show. We also had on stage one of the most successful comedies of our company, written and directed by Alexis and produced by me, with the title My Sexual Robot, which had been in a completely sold-out and full theater for about nine months. It looked like another of the plays that would be playing for a long time in

Miami's theaters. But the pandemic, like a ruthless jailer, closed the doors of all our homes and swallowed the keys indefinitely. Pharmacies, hospitals, and supermarkets were open, no one wanted to go outside. We were afraid to breathe any air that was not in our home, so we started doing the television program from home. It was one of the first programs that was broadcast that way during the critical months of confinement on Hispanic television in Florida; what a team of 10 people, including producers, writers, cameramen, and editors, would usually do, Alexis and I had to do by ourselves for the most part.

We started trying to do Zoom interviews with a lot of famous artists, and we recorded the scripts... For the first time, we were without any help, just the three of us at home, Lucía Alexis, and I locked up and producing a program with the particularity of being humorous. A difficult task in those times, isn't it? But as all chaos has its magic, it was in those days that Lucia really began to spread out her butterfly wings, and she had no other choice.

The therapists stopped coming—well, really, at that time, and for a few months, a lot of people stopped visiting our house—so we managed to do everything between the three of us. When Alexis and I were filming, Lucia spent most of her time on the floor, meaning she had to find a way to get what she wanted because I couldn't watch her 24 hours a day. We had to produce a daily program that we would also record and edit almost entirely ourselves. So, since neither mom nor grandmother (because my mom was at home only for a few days, and so was my mother-in-law) were not there, Lucía began from one day to the next to move alone on the floor, in her own way, crawling first, as if she were in a trench. I had read quite a bit about the topic of crawling and how important it is for children to somehow go through their different stages before walking. Generally, the first crawl usually begins between eight and 10 months. Still, every baby is different, so we shouldn't worry if our little one starts crawling before or after those ages. But Lucía was already more than a year and a half old; at that age, she should've been crawling already and, in the best of cases, walking.

When I saw her get to the things she wanted in this weird position, I remembered one of the many things I've read about the types of crawling that children commonly do.

Classic crawling on hands and knees or cross-crawling — The baby puts his or her weight on his or her hands and knees, then moves one arm and the opposite knee forward at the same time.

Bear crawling — It looks like classic crawling, but the baby keeps elbows and knees straight, using the hands and feet like a bear.

"Commando" crawling — The baby moves his or her body forward while dragging the belly against the floor.

Seated crawling — The baby slides on the buttocks and uses the arms to move forward.

Crab crawl — The baby moves backward or sideways like a crab, using the hands for propelling.

Rolling crawling — The baby arrives at its destination by rolling from one place to another.

Lucía started doing commando-type crawling, which would describe how soldiers move when they slide under trenches, and within a few days, she started doing rolling crawling. All by herself! It was very encouraging for us to see how she left her comfort zone, the zone in which everyone around her put things within her reach without knowing that effort would be the fundamental motivation to start the beautiful path of walking. In just a few weeks, Lucia began to gain the strength required for her arms and legs to be able to crawl in the classic way, that is, crawling on her hands and knees.

The days went by, and we were getting used to this new way of life, locked up, which fortunately would be temporary, but which seemed eternal at the time.

One day, while I was making breakfast, Lucia began to crawl perfectly, with hands and feet crossed. I couldn't believe it, which for some parents may be the most natural act in their child's life, for me, that she crawled like this, the way most children do, was one of my daughter's greatest achievements. I remember calling Alexis; I literally screamed, "Dad, run! Lucia is crawling!" It was an astonishment for everyone because we had always heard that crawling was the prelude to walking, so now we were very close. We had achieved one of our many goals. She had done it late, but she did it.

So here comes the conclusion of the beginning of this chapter.

Light A Match:

What seemed to be chaos for the whole world substantially changed my daughter's life. The pandemic, that monster unknown to most and unimaginable to everyone, brought to my house the need for Lucía to crawl. It took us out of our comfort zone, reinventing us, each in our own way, because many of us lost our jobs, which made us create new mechanisms to earn a living. It unleashed our imaginations to the max and unearthed hidden talents we may not have even known we had. It encouraged entrepreneurs to start their own small businesses and gave us the confidence to believe in resilience and reinvention, and for my daughter, it gave her strength to believe in her hands and feet. Because when you have no other choice, you must try all the options. Putting her face down, alone (of course always under surveillance) and with all the toys or food far away, and with mom and dad working without being able to keep up, made her try alone, as we say, "to make a living "by herself.

So, what may seem at first the worst moment of your existence will soon be one of the paths that lead you to discover who you are today, how strong you are, and above all, what you are capable of.

Chapter VIII

SEARCHING FOR ANSWERS

After the storm comes the calm, it's a saying we repeat, but we're rarely aware of how accurate it is. After the pandemic, life went back to normal, but with minor alterations, as you might expect. I think it injected us all with atomic fuel to have to face the fears our projects usually come with. And Lucía was and is my most ambitious project. Therefore, the fears that it generated and continues to generate in me are getting bigger and bigger.

Why a project?

I looked it up in the dictionary, and this is its definition:

Project: *(noun)*

1. "The idea of a thing which is intended to be done, and for which a definite mode and a set of necessary means are established."

In other words, Lucía is my reality turned into the most ambitious project I could have because I have the mission of looking for the necessary set of means for my beautiful project to advance and be, in its own way, imperfectly perfect, a difficult path when there is so much that we do not know, but nothing is impossible if you have Faith and Will. It's not that I have too much of either, but I do have immense love and absolute confidence in everything my daughter can achieve.

Soon, therapies returned to our lives. What a blessing! This time, I started taking her to the therapies four times a week, three hours of therapy each day, occupational, speech, and physical therapy, an intense program. It was like a little school, where you must be punctual and try not to miss, with the difference that, if you are absent, it does not affect your record, like when we were in elementary school, but it can affect the continuous development of our children.

For most parents, the therapies stage is very difficult, especially when they are carried out outside the home because they require a great personal effort and that of the family. For three or four hours of the day, our time will have to adjust like the gear of a clock to do the impossible to keep them in time. The key is consistency, ensuring that children with special needs miss as little as possible.

We must do magic, literally, to ask for favors at work. I know that there are mothers and fathers who find it very difficult, especially because most of the time, they don't have help, they are far from their families, and they lack the luck of a grandfather, a grandmother, or an aunt who will do the favor of taking the children. To which is added the days when we feel bad. Did you know that mothers get sick, too? Yes, we get sick too, although since Lucía was born, I hardly get sick. I think my body knows it can only break when there's no other option.

Whichever way you look at it, it's a huge challenge. We are forced to juggle to ensure that the mechanism of our routines does not affect that of our children and to readjust everything; that's what it's all about, isn't it? Go the extra mile to achieve the goal, like athletes. That's what parents with autistic children or other diagnoses become: athletes who need endurance, speed, and a lot of strength, physical, mental, and above all, emotional.

At the stage in question, a new therapist joined the team that was caring for Lucia, and that person became another big part of my salvations. His name is Ernesto, and I mention him in this book because I know that surely there are many therapists out there like him, wonderful and full of dedication and love for their work and for children, but for me, he will always be very special: he taught Lucía to walk.

Chapter IX

FLYING WITH YOUR OWN WINGS

When Lucía took her first steps, it was as if she drew the ground with each step, as if rays of light of all colors came out of her little toes, blinding those of us who incredulously watched her advance.

There, I understood that what for many is the most common, like walking, running, and jumping, for others, is something with an enormous level of complexity. The coordination it takes for one foot to move and then the other, the balance so as not to fall. The movement of the hands in the opposite movement to the foot that is resting at that moment, all this we do unconsciously, and it is natural.

But for many children, it requires more effort. I didn't know this. I didn't know how important physical therapy can be until my daughter started doing just the opposite of what that orthopedist said: walking.

By the end of August 2020, Lucía was already taking little steps, first two, then three, until, with a lot of patience, she began to walk on her own. Of course, she also began to discover the world of possibilities that came with this new skill.

Recently, I was watching some videos that her therapist sent me of when she took her first steps; she looked like a little drunkard walking with her hands up because that's how she managed to balance. "She must have been scared," I said to myself as I looked at the images over and over again. Lucía has always understood everything. I'm sure that children understand everything from a very young age, and maybe in some of our conversations, she learned about our fears.

Sometimes, we think that if we talk in front of children when they are very young, they will not understand us, which is a mistake. They understand everything and can also intuit when we are afraid or sad; in their own way, they process that information and surely generate scares in which they do not know how to swim.

That's why I try to be very careful about what I say in front of Lucia and how I behave. And that's why I celebrate every goal she goes over so that she knows that she's doing well, that she's doing better than many people thought, and that she's doing it as only Lucia can do.

So, I also want to thank Ernesto, the therapist mentioned in the previous chapter, and all the therapists who, like him, make it possible to achieve even the impossible from anonymity.

I don't think they are yet aware of the magic done with each of their therapies, nor how they teach us, parents, to push and push, even if the child doesn't want to do it, to keep trying and redirecting their effort until they understand that if they don't finish that exercise, they won't play or won't move on to the next one that is perhaps more fun because it requires less physical effort.

Therapists like Ernesto don't let kids give up, and that's just the kind of energy and perseverance that make a huge difference.

Before Lucía learned to walk, I often stared blankly, so Alexis asked me, "What are you thinking about?" "Nothing", I would answer back, but it wasn't true. I was really visualizing walking through the neighborhood with Lucía by the hand as my neighbor used to do almost every day with her little son. I imagined that we were running on the sidewalk, and I shouted at her, "Watch out for the almonds on the floor. You might fall!); I dreamed of stopping her because of how fast she was running and that it could be dangerous (we mothers see danger everywhere) ... That's what I was thinking about, something as simple as walking the distance from one corner to another hand in hand with Lucia.

Now we could do it, and I wouldn't have to stand at the window watching my neighbor go by.

All the time, I get these impulses that I must control for various reasons. One is that I'm an adult, and adults are expected to have a certain kind of moral and social etiquette that we all like to fit into, and that's why I resist the powerful impulse to go to the office of that orthopedist who claimed that my daughter would never be able to walk, open the door in one fell swoop and tell Lucía to do what I normally lecture her not to do: Let her run in, knocking down everything she sees in her path, and get to the desk full of files and say to that man: "Look, you, come and run with me, but fasten your shoelaces because you won't be able to catch up with me!"

Yes, that's what Alexis and I wanted to do, and more, to teach that man a lesson so that he learns that a diagnosis cannot be given as an absolute prognosis. I can't even imagine how many parents there must be out there broken-hearted by his sentencing their children to the impossibility of walking based only on his "learned opinion." But I didn't, and I don't think I will because I found a better way to get the urge to break into his office: this book.

This is more powerful as a weapon to fire a bullet of hope at those who deserve to receive this lesson, and it is not him; it is you, mothers and fathers, who read me. And the lesson is:

Light A Match

Never let them tell you what your child can or can't do, don't let anyone limit them. No one knows what your son or daughter will be, and only you will know when he or she shows it to you. Give them the opportunity and the confidence.

Chapter X

According to the Results...

Lucía's progress was evident. We were thrilled and proud, especially because of her impressive intelligence.

Did I mention Lucía's shocking photographic memory? I think I missed this important detail. Like many children with her "characteristics," she is brilliant. Her ability to learn at an inexplicable speed is almost supernatural.

At just six months old, she identified more than 30 animals; I remember that I bought her a package with all the animals from a farm, from the sea, and from the air. They were made of cardboard with rubber foam, and you could see the eyes and the little mouth protruding. They were very didactic toys. I only had to tell Lucia the name of the animal with the letter in front of her once, and this was enough for her to learn it without hesitation to identify them forever. Since she didn't speak yet, when I asked her, she would answer by pointing. That's how she did everything: the numbers, the alphabet, the geometric figures, everything, even the trapezoid or the heptagon, the colors, the flags of the countries. And when she started talking, it was even more impressive. Watching her identify more than 100 flags of countries I don't even know about, like Lithuania, Kazakhstan, Libya, Saudi Arabia, and Slovakia, she learned everything in one go! Who would be able to photograph everything and keep it forever in memory? Intelligence is also like memory, and Lucia has it, and she continues to impress us all with it.

Maybe that's why she also shows the ability to learn songs just by listening to them once; she is very in tune when she sings; she tries to find the exact note, and if she doesn't, she tries again. She has a completely musical ear, and she loves music deeply.

Before Lucia was diagnosed, I used to wonder what neurologists and psychologists used to say when a child was autistic, and since life has always been kind to me, I soon had the answer.

When she was two years and a few months old, we took Lucía to a new neurologist after going through three that had not convinced us. I'm not going to waste my time or yours telling you about my negative experience with those doctors. I'll sum it up with what my intuition as a mother told me: that they weren't the right ones for my daughter. And since a mother's intuition never fails, I let myself be guided once again by my life-saving pediatrician and went to Dr. Corrales, a very experienced child neurologist who turned the sails of our ship and directed it to a safer and more reliable port.

We drove for an hour and 30 minutes to get to his office under a tremendous downpour; maybe that's why we took longer than necessary; the truth is that I would drive that distance every day if I were to see doctors like him with so much knowledge, with so much dedication and kindness.

At the office, he asked me a few questions about Lucía. He asked how my pregnancy had been, if the birth was natural or by cesarian section, and if there had been any complications during gestation... But what caught my attention the most was the chart he made for us to understand how psychological evaluations work and the relationship it has with all neurological behavior in children.

He explained to me in depth about the term autism, and that's when I realized that I really knew very little or almost nothing about this neurodevelopmental condition.

Fear of the unknown is normal, especially when there are so many stigmas in society about certain diagnoses or topics that we don't really master until we are lucky enough to have an autistic child in the family.

At that time, at first glance, it was evident that Lucía had certain atypical neuro behaviors (it has rained a lot since then), but at that time, she did not speak, she had less eye contact, she still did not show confidence to walk many steps without falling, the first impression expressed by Dr. Corrales focused on the fact that the girl could be on the autism spectrum. Perhaps he saw my face of terror, because of my ignorance, and explained to me about this huge world, the immeasurable universe that exists within the autism spectrum. It's so big that if it was difficult for him as a specialist doctor to explain it, imagine for me. But I'll try to tell it just as my brain understands it and, above all, as my heart processes it.

Imagine a galaxy. Galaxies are clumps of gas, dust, and billions of stars and their solar systems, brought together by gravity. We live on a planet called Earth, which is part of our solar system and part of the Milky Way, which is our galaxy.

Well, imagine that this Galaxy is called the "Autism Spectrum" and that the millions of stars that make it up are the children diagnosed within the spectrum.

The spectrum is as big as a galaxy, and within its orbit are all kinds of typical and atypical behaviors that are used to determine the degree of complexity of our child, which can be mild, moderate, or severe. A galaxy is huge, isn't it? And besides, it is tough for us to know all the planets, stars, and solar systems that make it up, right? Well, the same happens with the autism spectrum. It is so immense that all diagnosed children act completely differently.

It is not something that is based on three or four clear or phenotypic specificities to help define this diagnosis. On the contrary, there are many components that can serve as a tool to discover if our little one is part of this huge galaxy.

The first way that allows us to determine it is by running tests, psychological tests composed of many questions that inquire into each activity that our children do or don't do, such as social behaviors, sensory problems, the notion of danger, reaction to stressful situations, cognitive level, development with their environment inside and outside the family.

Diagnosing autism spectrum disorders can be difficult because there is no medical test, such as a blood test, to prove it. To make a diagnosis, doctors evaluate the child's development and behavior.

Do you remember when I used to ask myself how children were diagnosed with autism? I already had my answer, through a questionnaire with hundreds of questions, which we, the parents, can answer better than anyone else. These questions will help you become more aware of your child's abilities and deficiencies because we often get used to their behaviors as we live with them all the time.

These questions were sometimes a little uncomfortable for me, especially when the answer was repeatedly "NO." I answered for my daughter many times the same questionnaires for different doctors or agencies that needed to get the diagnosis; over and over again, I answered the same questions, and over and over again, it affected me a lot when the answer was still NO.

This stage was hard for me; if I'm writing this book, it's to tell the truth, and my truth is that the first few times, some questions caused me to cry uncontrollably. Does your son or daughter call you mom? Can he/she make conversation with you or a child or adult in his environment? Does your child say more than five words? Does your child understand when you're sad? For a long time, the answers to those tests were No, and the simple fact of checking that option, that adverb of negation so common to everyone, took me hours to assimilate and understand why my answer could not be Yes.

The first time I answered these questions on a website, I had to stop. I left them unfinished for two days, it is not the same to know that your son or daughter cannot do certain things yet than to internalize them by answering questions that I had not asked myself before, at least not so consciously.

In those two days of avoiding answering those questions, I went alone to a place that always gives me, with its peace, the answers I need most: the sea.

There, in front of the blue water, I sat for several hours alone, in silence, without emotions or fears, just me and the sound of the water that wet my feet, and as if by magic, my brain opened a lock that blocked many of my most unknown feelings and tied my greatest strength, willpower, which is capable of flying in seconds. Of breaking walls, of moving mountains, the one that is always accompanied by one of my favorite words: Faith.

I remember that day; it was evening, the horizon turning reddish and yellow, and the light was beautiful, like a scene from a Sarah Polley movie. For a few seconds and as if in fast motion, I went with my imagination through the interior of homes where, at that very moment, there was an autistic child. I saw their mothers' faces and their fathers' eyes. I realized that we were in a huge sea full of fish of different colors, a galaxy, and I was a part of that. I felt that I had a huge and very delicate responsibility: to help my daughter reach the limit of her possibilities and, if possible, beyond.

I went home, didn't say hello, and went straight to my computer, the same I'm writing this book for you right now. I sat down, opened the question page, and answered everything in one go, with no adjacent emotions to make me stop. Let's get on with it and do what we must now, right?

And we came to move forward, succeed, and leave deep marks on everything around us. My daughter couldn't wait for me, and I didn't have the right to be worthless; every second that passed would play against me; the faster I placed myself with Lucía in this new world, the greater her advancement would be. Was it partly up to me? All that was and is necessary on my part, it was and will be done.

Why cry? Why postpone? Neither tears nor the delay in my time would make a positive difference in her.

Ready! Once the questions were answered, we had the result, which we already intuited but which is always moving to note.

"Your child is on the autism spectrum. According to the results, your child is autistic, to a moderate degree..."

In my head, this phrase plays like a recording over and over, as if I am pressing the *stop* and *play* button again and again.

How is it possible that something you already know can surprise you? Emotions are hard for neuroscientists to explain; for me, they are almost indescribable. I know that my mind and my whole being accepted this diagnosis without any resistance. Do you know why? I had already learned something from this experience with this heartbreaker orthopedic, diagnoses are not prognostic, let alone labels.

CHAPTER XI

'IN YOUR SHOES...

I'm not here to tell you what to do about your child or how to do it. Nobody can dictate how our hearts and brains react to certain news. I tell my experiences because at the time, I also needed to read something like this that came from a mother, not from a psychologist who is used to dealing with problems or concerns from a neutral space.

I'm in your shoes, walking beside you, and I know it's hard, especially considering how diverse and huge this spectrum is. I understand that many mothers and fathers have to deal with our situations differently; some cases are very severe, many others must live with medication for seizures, there are aggressive children, and all this falls on families like a roulette wheel, randomly.

Most of us parents have to juggle a daily plan, therapies, consultations, and work, leaving aside the individual part, living only to understand and discover how to help our children move forward.

I also know the grief and despair that sometimes comes from facing everything that is out of the "normal." Sometimes, it helps a lot to feel like we belong to something, to a huge group that shares the same interests and similar concerns. Although it is a bit of a selfish feeling, knowing that we are not alone on this boat, feeling accompanied, is also a way of feeling protected.

Commenting on our experiences helps us identify solutions that have meant significant changes for others or discard alternative treatments that don't work. The important thing is to share, give, and receive valuable information, and it could make a big difference for many parents who feel lost or alone.

There are three things that have relieved me a lot.

Light A Match

-Don't blame yourself

-Don't judge yourself

-Don't give up

I'm talking about guilt in the first place because I've experienced it a lot in motherhood, and we have to learn to live without that daily feeling of judging ourselves for everything that happens around us, of blaming ourselves for everything that doesn't go perfectly. Guilt, like complaining, is sterile. Neither brings anything positive. Of course, as we are human, all feelings are valid, but we have to learn to define how and when we can afford to feel them, and this is not the case because really nothing that is happening has originated by you or by me, or by anything to which responsibility should be attributed. This is not the time to look for culprits but to find solutions.

If it's any consolation, I also sometimes feel like crying, I feel out of place, and I question if I'm doing it right, but I don't let that feeling of eternal responsibility for everything manage me.

I close my eyes, and I hold the hands of all the mothers who are in this tide of so many colors, which for some has been a calmer sea and for others a storm. I squeeze their hands and transmit all the positive energy that we often need. It is not that I have too much of it, but I can share the beauty that I find along the way. And if that will help at least one person, then I will. There are many of us swimming in this ocean.

Secondly, I used the word judge, because it's an action verb that we often use, sometimes unknowingly, and can be very cruel. This is another of the lessons that Lucia has brought me. With her, I learned that for some, what can be solved or done in seconds can take considerable time for others, and that does not make them less capable.

My personality, for example, is agile; I try to look for quick and practical solutions for almost everything that comes my way. I am always coming up with things, but many people around me are not like that, and before I made the mistake of despairing and again judging people who did not understand me at first, and life, as a good and wise teacher, it made me understand that I was wrong and, in addition, I have been very unfair and sometimes ruthless.

That is why I also want to offer apologies through these pages, in case, due to my ignorance, I did not have the calmness to accept that each person has his or her own rhythm to react, understand, and abide by things, for not respecting the times of others on some occasions, for thinking "Geez, You're slow" of someone to whom I had to repeat something more than once.

I'm sure we've all had that moment of intolerance towards other people, in a restaurant, with a waiter who got the order wrong, on a plane with someone who is late putting their things down, at school when a classmate asked the same question many times simply because they didn't understand, we've all felt in some way that need to rush the other who is going slower than us.

Now, we can correct that urge to try and label and assume that we can all think at the same speed by being aware of everyone's individuality, that we all do what we can in the best possible way, and by stopping judging, by understanding once and for all that the other may be having a very bad time at that moment. If all children were raised with this precept, the next generations would be filled with understanding, compassion, inclusion, and respect.

They say that children come with a loaf of bread under their arms. Besides having a loaf of bread under her arms, I have always thought Lucia also came with a mirror. For the first time since she was born, I really looked into it, saw myself, and discovered who I was and what I was capable of. Maybe that's what you need too, to look at yourself in the mirror, to really look at yourself, to find the shield that we are all born with, but that many times we don't know how to take out or when because it's useless to have tools if we don't know when to use them.

Strength, decisiveness, and courage are like instruction manuals. What's the point of having one with all the steps if it's in a language we don't know? That is why we must prepare a lot and put it all together: strength, decision, and courage, with a fourth ingredient that will make the path more passable: information.

Without information, we go through life almost naked. Fortunately, today, there are countless sources with everything you need to know and more. This has been another weapon to gain ground in this battle, to read a lot, not everything, but a lot, to search tirelessly, and as a detective, to find all the information out there that neither doctors nor experts in the field tell us, that only we, the parents of children with autism or with some special diagnosis can find.

Of course, many times, we embrace any alternative method as if it were a visa to get out of autism, and this is a completely understandable and, to some extent, necessary attitude, but a lot of information can also confuse us.

I've seen myself several times starting books that I honestly leave halfway, with remedies, diets, or methods that, in the end, I don't even know if I should try with my daughter, everything that goes through her mouth, or everything that doesn't go in is my responsibility, so you can understand how pressured I can feel sometimes, that's why I stopped reading medical books about autism and started believing in my own intuition.

There is one method that has never failed me and that I must recommend to you without any doubt: LOVE.

Chapter XII

CONVERSATION WITH ANOTHER MOTHER LIKE ME

There are words or phrases that hurt. It hurts to hear them, perhaps because they are loaded with a cultural burden that affects their true meaning. Sometimes, those words spoken with the wrong intention can lacerate our mother's heart. Due to its lack of knowledge, society can be very cruel at times, although I have already learned to forgive certain questions and words because I know that they are not said with bad intentions but from ignorance. This is the part of the wrong narrative: Children viewed as
'Children with problems:'

Disable

Delayed

Retarded

Special Needs...

And many others that I spare because the mere fact of writing them clouds my heart. But if I stand on the other side of the sidewalk, from the position of a person who knows nothing about autism or syndromes, diagnoses related to hyperactivity or dyslexia, if I cross the street, I who have also been on that side before Lucía was born, then I may be able to understand the curiosity aroused by the unknown.

Without pretending to give lessons to anyone, I want to suggest to those who read me and sometimes do not know how to refer to our autistic children or those with any syndrome, that they try to use less aggressive terms or that in some way they can hurt sensitivities, especially us, the mothers of children on the autism spectrum, who are more likely to feel deeply dismayed when certain denominations are used towards them. That although they are not said with bad intentions but out of ignorance, they can make us sad or create uncomfortable situations. That is why I invite you to use the word **neuro divergence** when referring to children on the spectrum.

The term neurodiversity originated in the 90s to fight the stigma of people with autism, as well as ADHD [3] and learning disorders such as dyslexia, Tourette's syndrome, dyspraxia, synesthesia, dyscalculia, epilepsy, bipolar disorder, and obsessive-compulsive disorder, among others.

Is it more comfortable and less hopeless to use this term? Yes! Is your original diagnosis going to change in any way by calling them one way or another? No! But if we can make a mom or a neurodivergent person feel better just by modifying the way we call or see them, then we are doing right by them, and maybe, in turn, this action will serve as another way to contribute to all of us integrating better into society.

Every human being is as unique as their fingerprint, and if we abide by that premise, then we are all different. What is the rule that sets the standard of "normalcy"? If we are all fundamentally different, what is it that makes us be guided by a certain parameter? I think society and that constant need to put a name to everything, but if we look at it from the positive side,

---

[3] Attention deficit hyperactivity disorder.

maybe labels are not as bad as they seem. Maybe they give us a reason, an answer.

That's how I felt with Nuria, the mother of Natalie, a 21-year-old girl who was diagnosed on the autism spectrum when she was almost an adult. Nuria spent her second daughter's entire childhood full of doubts. Natalie was not like the rest of the children, not even like her older sister, but at that time, in 2000, there was not so much information about autism, so Nuria went to many consultations with different doctors looking for answers that she found almost 18 years later.

I met Natalie at the horse therapies I take my daughter to. And here, I'm going to make a parenthesis to tell you a little bit about this very positive addition to my daughter's life. Equine therapy is another important match in its little box. We started them when Lucía was three years old, and the progress in many aspects was noticeable from the first class. Equine therapy is considered comprehensive because it positively impacts cognitive, physical, emotional, social, and occupational development.

Equine therapy is recommended for people with mental, physical, or sensory disabilities, for people with psychological, language or learning disorders and also for people with problems of marginalization or social maladjustment. It can be used by both adults and children, also in early stimulation.

Among the physical benefits of equine therapy are the development of muscle tone by working several muscles at the same time, the increase in strength, endurance, balance, and coordination, and the improvement of motor dexterity. So, if you have the possibility to bring your son or daughter, do not hesitate to do so. The bond of friendship that horses and humans create is beautiful and unique.

Let's go back to the protagonists of this chapter, Nuria and Natalie. The day we met was very special because Natalie's father came up to me to greet me and tell me that he had coincidentally studied with my father at the University, that he remembered him very fondly, and that because of that endearing memory, he dared to be daring and talk to me about the courage with which he always sees me when I am with my daughter. That he had a grown daughter who had just been diagnosed with autism and Asperger's and that something told him that I should meet her. She took me to her, and I saw a beautiful girl, fragile at first glance and with a look that reminded me a lot of Lucia's, the kind of look that settles on you and pierces your soul with eyes that speak for themselves. We talked for a few minutes, and then the word depression came up. I recommended that she listen to an episode of my podcast dedicated to depression, which I was sure would help her a lot. We exchanged phone numbers and agreed that he would come to see one of my plays at the theater.

That day, I couldn't get it out of my head, while at the same time, I began to visualize what Lucía would be like at the age of 20; my imagination shot up, and so did my fears. I wanted to meet her mother, I thought at that moment that it would help me a lot to hear her story and process as a mother of a special girl. So, I contacted her, and she gave me a valuable Zoom chat that I will try to transcribe here.

My first question was:

—"How did you know Natalie was different?"

—"When Natalie was a baby, she didn't crawl like other children. She did it in a different way, she started walking very late, almost when she was three years old, she didn't speak, she was very repetitive in her movements, and you have to remember that at the time Natalie was born there wasn't so much information about autism, but I always knew that Natalie was on the spectrum, even though I didn't know at the time that it was called that way. At school, it was hard for her to advance in class; she could barely write her name. The teacher always complained to me that Natalie got lost looking at the ceiling and that she didn't pay attention, but the most worrying thing was when it came to socializing with the other children."

These were some of the light bulbs that illuminated in Nuria the idea that Natalie could be autistic. As the girl was so far behind compared to her classmates, her parents looked for a tutor who began to work individually and rigorously on the same classes taught at school. She went every day in the afternoon, so Natalie was learning all day, and in three weeks, an incredible change was noticed: She began to make impressive progress in school.

But Natalie had a hard time making friends. Despite being a very sweet, charming, and affectionate girl, developing that social side was difficult.

I was very interested to know how Nuria and everyone at home had taken the fact of receiving a diagnosis of autism when her daughter was already an adult, this was her response:

—"Natalie was diagnosed on the autism spectrum at the age of 21. You'll be amazed at what I'm going to tell you, Claudia. When she was diagnosed, I felt relieved because my mom's heart had already told me, and what I wanted was a check-up so that everyone at home, and especially her, would understand exactly what she had and how we could help her. This diagnosis has helped her a lot to understand her behavior and why it was so hard for her to have friends or to keep up with school. It was a relief."

Nuria told me that her daughter learned to imitate what other girls did in order to try to integrate with her classmates. *Starting middle school*[4] was one of the strongest changes she had to face for Natalie; it was the stage of parties and outings; many of her classmates did not invite her, and if they invited her, then she did not know if she wanted to go.

I confess that at this point in the conversation, I felt a little afraid, thinking about when that moment would come for Lucía, but Nuria calmed me down when she told me something that I will never forget and— I want it to serve as a **Match** for you **to Light**:

"Don't be afraid because you're more prepared. I wish I'd known all this that you already know when Natalie

---

4 Middle school for sixth through eighth grades.

was Lucia's age. If I had been certain of that diagnosis since she was little, I think she would have been more prepared, she would have had less frustration."

And she's right; I've already learned how to deal with everything since she was very little. I haven't tired of seeking information and advice, and I won't get tired.

We also talk about guilt, which is something that has always caught my attention, that generates a lot of doubts, and that recurrence of feeling guilty. I wanted to know if she felt it, too, and what her stance or vision was on that. Nuria told me that she always wondered where she went wrong as a mother that she couldn't realize before, but that getting closer to God has been a huge source of peace and helped her to understand that things happen to acquire a lesson and that all this has made her a stronger woman, capable of facing things that she would not have been able to before. Natalie brought home strength, togetherness, and faith. Talking to other moms and sharing experiences has also been fundamental for Nuria. She told me that Natalie has been admitted to the hospital many times with anxiety attacks and suicidal thoughts, and just on some of those occasions, in a way, it was a relief to meet other families who are going through similar situations.

—"How does a mother sit with her adult son or daughter to explain that he or she is autistic?"

—"It's a long process," Nuria told me. "Natalie is very smart. When she was in her first year of *college*, which was when the most worrisome crises began, she herself began to look for information to try to understand why she was different and concluded that she had autism.

One of the times she was hospitalized, she called me on the phone and said, "Mommy, the doctor talked to me. "What I have is mild autism and I'm obsessive-compulsive." And she expressed it to me so calmly that even I couldn't understand it myself. In Natalie's case, it wasn't a problem for her to assimilate. On the contrary, it was like a relief. The fact that she was diagnosed so late deprived us of the possibility of my daughter receiving therapy as a child. We have had a lot of problems finding therapies for adults, there are not many, and at her age she is always sent to a psychologist. In fact, perhaps the therapies with horses were the most positive, especially at the beginning."

—"What's your plan at home with Natalie when she's older?"

—"The plan is for her to be happy. Maybe it's difficult, but that's our goal: for her to have peace of mind, for her to love herself, for her to become more independent. Something very important is that here in the family, her dad, her sister, and I are a team. The family is the center, if they don't have support, there is no progress. Natalie has accomplished so much because she has us, because we are always together, supporting her, understanding her, or at least trying to do so."

—"What's your biggest fear as a mom?" (This was the question that caused me the most anxiety, because I was sure that his answer would be the same as mine, and so it was.)

—"That she can't fend for herself, that it's hard for her to become independent. I don't like to think about it, but sometimes I fear for her when I'm gone."

—"What would you say to parents who are facing an autism diagnosis right now?"

— "Accept the diagnosis, seek help, the sooner, the better, take them to therapy, that there is family unity, never be ashamed of having an autistic child, on the contrary, for me, it is a blessing to give them love, a lot of love, when there is love everything is possible, do not give up and never lose faith."

CHAPTER XIII

DR. CORRALES, OUR NEUROLOGIST.

One of the fundamental reasons for writing this book is to pass on the information, the lots of it, or the little that I find, so I asked the doctor who diagnosed my daughter to give me an hour of his time to answer some of the many questions that run through my head.

We also chatted via Zoom. It was hard to find the time because he is always seeing patients. His only available time was his lunchtime. That is why I am very grateful for the kindness of Dr. Corrales, who stopped eating lunch that day to give us some of his information and knowledge for this book.

Here is our conversation in its entirety.

"What's autism?"

"Autism is a syndrome characterized by several developmental deficits: deficits in verbal and nonverbal communication, deficits in social interaction, repetitive restrictive behaviors, and sensory disorders. Communication has several parts; verbal communication, for example, one understands language and expresses one's ideas, which can be in the case of the young child in words, or after 24 months in small sentences, we repeat, we read, and we write. These are the parts of spoken language; there are two other parts that are learned later, reading and writing, and the first three parts are learned at home. But language also has a non-verbal component, which has a lot to do with reciprocity between two individuals, such as responding to your name. Children on the autism spectrum don't respond well to their name."

"When should a child start responding to their name?"

"Usually around twelve months. Another important part is to point with the index finger; indicating is very important because when you can't communicate verbally, and that is experienced when you go to other countries with other languages, and you don't understand, then you use the index finger lot to communicate. In our Western society, the index finger is vital for signaling your needs or for indicating things you want someone else to look at. For example, when we see an airplane, we usually point to the airplane so that our children can see it, or the child points it to us, saying he doesn't want the airplane; he is making you part of that social reciprocity of "I want you to see what I'm seeing." Other crucial points include eye contact, pointing, responding with a gesture to your name, greeting, saying goodbye, and having that reciprocity of staying on the same topic. Many children on the autism spectrum, for example, change the topic. We call it "tangential conversations." They talk a lot about restrictive topics, such as dinosaurs, trains, animals, and birds, and in all the talks, they want to talk about that. I often ask the parents, "When you talk to your child, does the topic of conversation change?" A lot of parents tell me that, yes, the kids redirect the conversation to where they feel comfortable. Now, there are cases in which communication is very affected, this child is non-verbal, does not understand or has a hard time understanding, does not follow instructions, and is not able to understand verbal communication with their parents sometimes they are moderate cases that with the help of gestures, cards can follow instructions such as "pick this up and put it there", "Sit here," "Bring me such and such. These are the four deficits that have to do with social interaction. For example, there are children on the spectrum who have a lot of difficulty initiating interaction; it is the child who, for example, goes to a party and does not integrate into the group or plays alone. There is also a severe case that is of children who do not recognize other children, which surely you have heard a lot out there about "living in their own world." There is also the child who, yes, establishes an interaction but snatches toys, and precisely part of the interaction has a lot to do with sharing; social interaction is very important, especially in the childhood stage, because it creates the basis of these social skills that you will need later in your adult stage, such as maintaining a relationship, a working relationship, etc. Sometimes, parents tell me that their children don't play with other children, or run with the other children, or jump down the slides, but this is a more parallel game. The game consists of several parts; first, we need to understand what we play; we must share and take turns, enjoy the game, and know why we're playing and what the purpose of the game is."

"To be diagnosed on the autism spectrum, do you necessarily have to have all four deficits, or is just one or two enough?"

"In theory, it should present deficits in the different areas. One that should always be present when diagnosing is the deficit in social interaction, for example, these children who invade the personal spaces of others and hug people even without knowing them. In my opinion, that is not something unfavorable because it can be modulated. Motor or flapping behaviors, or stereotypes when it comes to moving the hands, are also things that arouse suspicion, walking in circles and turning lights on and off. About *stimming* (which consists of repetitive movements), there are several theories related to areas in the brain that are poorly connected. We know what the areas of spoken language are: There are two areas in the dominant hemisphere: for right handed people, is the left hemisphere, and for left-handed people, it lies in the right hemisphere. These areas oversee language: Broca's area, which is involved in language production, and Wernicke's area, in word comprehension. We have trillions of neurons that communicate with each other through tiny antennae called dendrites. Many studies have been done and it is thought that in the brains of autistic children they remain less connected than in the neurotypical child. There is, for example, another very common characteristic of autism, which is echolalia, a speech disorder that consists of the involuntary and unconscious repetition of words, phrases, snippets of conversation, songs that the child has heard from people close to him. There's also the child who has a robotic language. For example, I've seen children learn lines from movies and use them in the right context, but it's a very far-fetched language, not used in colloquial language."

"What causes autism?"

"There are several theories, genetic theories, structural theories in the brain, there is also talks of obstetric complications, of the mother during pregnancy, childbirth, for example, is much more frequent in the premature child, the child born before 36 or 37 weeks. It also appears in mothers with diseases during pregnancy such as hypertension, preeclampsia, eclampsia, both gestational diabetes and type 1 or type 2 diabetes. So, it is very important during pregnancy to properly treat hypertension and diabetes. There has also been talk of infections during pregnancy, simple infections, of which three infections have been related to autism, congenital rubella, cytomegalovirus, and herpes simplex type 1 or type 2. Since there are some genetic syndromes associated with autism, I really like to send my patients for genetic testing, especially when they are young parents who are thinking about having another child, so that they can receive genetic counseling in their family planning. I also want to tell you that, yes, you can, and I always like to speak in my office with positivity because most children with autism get better; the earlier the diagnosis is established, the faster they can be helped. My dilemma as a neurologist is that I want to help autistic children. Still, I don't have what the pediatrician has, which is a treatment for when they have, for example, an ear infection, which heals in 10 days, while developmental disorders are more chronic. My best help is to refer them to therapy because therapies are never going to hurt anyone."

"Are there any theories that point to the relationship between vaccines and autism? Can you tell me a little bit about that?"

"Vaccines have been linked to autism for a long time. Vaccines were preserved with Thimerosal to prevent germs, bacteria, or fungi from contaminating them, and thimerosal has mercury, a heavy metal, so it was theorized that there could be a link between it and autism. The issue is that thimerosal was removed from vaccines in 2006 or 2007, but the incidence of autism continued to increase during those years. Studies were done by vaccines, and it was found how much mercury is harmful to humans and that mercury per vaccine was not enough to cause harm, although the cumulative effect of all the vaccines was almost at the limit of causing organ damage, and even then, after the mercury was removed, the incidence continued to rise. There is no confirmed relationship, studies have even been done in countries with social medicine, such as those in Europe. One vaccine has been heavily mixed up with autism in some theories: the one-year-old vaccine called MMR, which fights measles, mumps, and rubella. Many parents do not want their children to be inoculated, but a comprehensive study conducted in Denmark found that there is no link between vaccines and autism[5]."

---

[5] This information can be found in the New England Journal of Medicine.

"What is your opinion about television and how much time cartoons should be allowed for children to watch?"

"There was a theory that existed long ago about it, based on this; "refrigerator parents" for being cold and incommunicable with their children, preferring to have them watch cartoons all day. But I don't think watching television produces autism. Maybe I'm not in favor of the super exposure of television for children. The American Association of Pediatrics has a website, www.aap.org, where you can create an account, and they recommend what is healthy according to the child's age. In my opinion, although it does not cause autism, I do not think it is healthy to spend many hours in front of the television. I see that addiction to the screen and to phones behaves like that of tobacco or alcohol. I believe that we do have to control, at the state or federal level, the average amount that our children consume."

"How do I know how the brain of a typical neurodivergent child differs from that of a neurodivergent one?"

"Most children with autism have a normal MRI, I particularly don't like to recommend MRIs and the reason is that the moment we diagnose children between 18 and 36 months to do this test on that child you have to sedate them. Put them to sleep, and I don't really like to do that unless there's something in the medical chart that tells me that if I have to do it, for example, the child who had a neonatal infection or the mother who had a neonatal infection, like this type of herpes or cytomegalovirus, or the child who had hypoxic-ischemic suffering, (hypoxia means low oxygen, ischemic that there is a lack of blood supply to the brain), because that baby who had a complication before, during or after labor, I prefer to check them well with an MRI. Now, at a functional level, they are different; there are areas that have little communication between neurons and others that are hyperconnected. When children come to the clinic, one of the first things we like to do is a hearing test because we want to be sure that the child can hear because if they don't, they can't respond to their name or anything. Generally, the child who is deaf and hard of hearing communicates very well non-verbally, establishes very good eye contact, points, and makes many hand gestures. The deaf child, for example, is going to have very good eye contact, and the child with autism looks like he is listening, but to a greater or lesser degree, he is going to have difficulties with these nonverbal skills to communicate, such as eye contact, pointing, greeting, responding to his name, among other aspects."

"How can you explain that some children on the autism spectrum can develop specific skills for math, or music, or memory? "

"I think it has to do with this physiological duck mechanism of many connections in some areas of the brain and disconnection in other areas. For example, I have had children who are geniuses in mathematics, I do think it has to do with this mechanism of hyper connection in some areas that they have with mathematics and disconnection with others related to interaction, communication. There are a lot of people who are considered geniuses who have symptoms that are very similar to autism. I think in the past they weren't diagnosed because maybe they were high-functioning kids and didn't need any intervention."

"What would you recommend to the mothers, fathers, and families in general of children on this spectrum?"

"I want to tell the parents that this condition not only affects the child, it affects the little brother, the mother, the grandparents, it affects the marriage, I see a lot of parents at the beginning together and then I begin to see less, for example the father, not in all cases of course, but it happens a lot, but I see a lot of separation of parents. When it is very important to be together because they are better off having Daddy and Mommy in a stable home, and I always recommend to parents that they sleep together, not to put the child in the bed of the couple because the couple has to be together to be able to help the son or daughter. We have to be positive. There is even a theory of not exposing them to medical treatments, I have parents who do not want therapies and that's fine, I like the theory of treating them with therapies because I want to give them the benefit of incorporating them into society, not neglecting them, but making them part of society. The important thing is to be positive because the children get better. Do we need to help them a little more? Yes, do we have to be on top of them? Yes. But that's what we're here for. The other thing is to raise them with love. I always tell parents that children are raised with two things: love and teaching them to have discipline, the two things together, you have to feel the love of your parents and also that your parents are teaching you, but always with love, a lot of love."

Talking with Dr. Corrales and Nuria helped me a lot. It calmed me down and somehow drew me a clearer path to follow as Lucía grows.

CHAPTER XIV

DIEGO INFANTE

It seemed unfair to write about autism and not hear firsthand about someone's experience on the spectrum. So, I started looking for a neurodivergent adult who could tell me about their experience, not a difficult task thanks to the advantage of having social networks at my fingertips.

In this case, Instagram was key. Searching with the hashtag #autista I found a huge community of autistic adults who seek to make neurodivergent people visible every day and from their experiences. I was very surprised; I didn't expect to come across such a united and interesting collective.

Among so many beautiful people, I met a university professor and father of an autistic girl, a pregnant occupational therapist, a beautiful actress, singer and director, a neuroscience specialist, a musician, a grandmother, all adults, with lives made and completely integrated into society, with professions, desires, aspirations, full knowledge and above all pride in their condition.

I started exchanging messages with everyone; I told them that as a mother, I needed to listen to them and know what their life had been like, what their biggest fears were, and what I could do as a mother to better understand my daughter. Their answers were more and more enlightening, and I managed to understand many of Lucía's reactions by learning from them.

One was recommending me to the other until I came to Diego Infante, a young Chilean autistic therapist and possibly one of the most tender and interesting people I have ever met in my life. Diego gave me, more than a revealing conversation, a real-life lesson, and I can't help but share his testimony as the greatest spark for all the matches we've kept in our box.

Here it goes.

—"How do you perceive the world? How do you see people?"

—"Autistic people, in general, are more sensitive; some are hypersensitive, and we feel everything more intensely; there are also hypersensitive people, who feel less, but the vast majority feel noises, smells, and textures more intensely. When we are on the street or in a place where there are many people, some of us feel a little overwhelmed. Sometimes, we get tired faster because we are more exposed to stimuli; we feel them more intensely, which makes us exhaust ourselves quickly; it is sensory fatigue, which tires us. I saw life as a wonderful thing when I was a child. I saw everything as a giant does; everything impressed me a lot, and then, as I grew up, I began to see things more as they are, sometimes just as bright, just as when I was a child. All that depends on how I am at any given moment. I received the diagnosis at a late age, at 25, because during my childhood, I knew very little about autism. Only those with very marked characteristics were diagnosed, but those who did not were diagnosed with other pathologies, such as personality disorders, depression, and even some schizophrenia until now when we are adults and more is known about autism, and we have been able to reach the official diagnosis, that's the most important thing."

—"How did you receive the diagnosis of autism?"

—"Since the age of eleven, I began to realize that I was different. For example, I had difficulties in communication when interacting with others and following instructions. However, I also noticed that I had and still have really good skills with numbers when doing mental calculations and remembering dates. When I was 23, I suffered an injury, tendonitis, to be more specific. Looking for a way to heal it, someone suggested a doctor who works with an ancient Chinese technique called Acupuncture. It turns out that there are many points in the body that, when pressed, have an energetic effect. So, they put needles on you, and each needle causes an effect. I started receiving the sessions, and I was getting better every day. One day, this acupuncturist commented that I seemed very smart, so I took the opportunity to ask him what he thought of my case, and he replied instantly he believed that it was a case of Asperger's. I should tell you here that the Asperger syndrome diagnosis is no longer very used. As I understand it, someone with Asperger was considered as a high-functioning autistic, but now that definition is not made, now it is measured depending on the level of therapeutic support that is required. Going back to my diagnosis, the acupuncturist told me on Monday, February 16, 2015, when I was 23 years and two months and 12 days old. He explained to me that Asperger's is not a disease but a condition, that we are a different type of people, we are structured, literal, detail-oriented people, passionate about some issues, that our great mission in life is to adapt to society and that society also has to adapt to us. I started researching and I came across several pages, in some of them, autistic families talk about autism from the third person and in others of autistic adults, there I began to feel more identified; I also met some autistics until I went for the diagnosis in 2017 when I was already 25 years old. This time, it was a neurologist who referred me to a neuropsychologist for the official diagnosis. On that occasion, I had to answer many tests, and with those results, the neurologist diagnosed me. That happened on Wednesday, August 2, 2017, when I was 25 years and seven months and 26 days old."

—"When you were diagnosed, how did you feel?"

—"The neurologist explained to me in a few words, the same as the acupuncturist. It was super helpful. She told me that most autistic people require therapy because of their hypersensitivity to touch, sight, and noises and that many cannot look into the eyes because it is very difficult for them; it was also difficult for me. Many autistic people have suffered from *bullying*,[6] and therapy is very important to heal. She expressed to me that all human beings have things to work on, whether or not they have this condition, and for me, it was very healing to say to myself, "I am different, but there is nothing wrong with it." For some years I didn't understand society very well, and as I grew up, I didn't understand myself either, now with this diagnosis I

---

[6] Bullying is aggression to exert power over another person.

could understand society and myself, and that's super liberating. I realized that I could have a completely normal life with some difficulties but that it wasn't a disease, so I felt very happy indeed."

—"When you were a child, did you speak early, or did it take you a while to start talking?"

—"At the age of two, I began to say the first words, and at three, I could already put together sentences, but they couldn't understand them. That happens a lot in autism; there are some who learn to speak even later, at five, six, and seven, and there are others who do not speak or end up speaking very late. The support of speech therapists is huge because they are the professionals in charge of speech, that is, language, including for non-verbal, who are unable to speak, for whom there are other tools to learn to communicate, such as pictograms, tables, and augmentative communication systems. Hence, the support of these professionals is very important. It is said that in the first seven years of life, there is greater brain plasticity, which is a very important reason to make a diagnosis as early as possible, therapies too, because, in those years, you can make a lot of progress. I started going to therapy at the age of five, not knowing that I was autistic; my family and the teachers at school knew about the difficulties I had, but without an official diagnosis. I suffered from a lot of vertigo of heights, I still have it, but I'm going to overcome that fear; in fact, I have an idea to overcome it."

—"How does an autistic person live?

"Personally, I like to be treated well, like any other person; I like for people around me to be flexible; if they see that I feel bad, they ask how I'm doing. The issue of bullying itself affects a lot of people, but much more so a neurodivergent who has a different condition or a minority group. I have heard, for example, cases of autistic people who are bullied at school and, sometimes, even the teachers themselves discriminate against them, perhaps out of ignorance. In my case, I didn't have any problems. Maybe there was a classmate who bothered me, but it didn't happen with the adults; something very curious in my case that almost never happens is that many times, those who bothered me when I was little ended up including me later on because they became aware that it was wrong to bully. But there was a stage in my life when I suffered a lot of bullying after I left school. Fortunately, or miraculously, I met someone who ended up becoming my psychologist, and with her therapy, I was able to get through that stage in a brilliant way. This psychologist also encouraged me to fight bullying."

—"I've heard a lot that most autistic people are very literal. Does that happen to you, too?"

—"It happened to me a lot, especially as a child; for example, sometimes we were talking about something, and I would say, "How nice? " and others would laugh because they found it ridiculous, and I would ask them, "Do you like it?" And they would say yes, sarcastically, of course, but I didn't register the sarcastic tone, so they laughed at what I found beautiful and didn't understand. People on the autism spectrum find it very difficult to recognize the emotions of others. We are very literal; for example, when someone makes a joke, it is difficult for those of us on the autistic spectrum to recognize if something is a joke or not to perceive the double intentions of the other person. Some people have bad intentions and show pretty faces, so you believe them when they have another intention. I have had to hear many stories, for example, of women on the autism spectrum. Female autism is less noticeable than male autism because many girls mask[7] to look like neurotypical people. Many autistic women have ended up in very violent relationships, and there is manipulation. In these instances, the man ends up being an aggressor and a manipulator because it just makes the autistic person think that she is sick, and so she lets herself be dominated."

—"How has your relationship been with your mom, dad, and your family?"

—"The relationship with my parents and sister has been good. For example, my mom has helped me a lot with the issue of vertigo and the fear of heights. When I was a child, she took me to therapy. Well, as a child, and when I was a teenager also because I had like two stages of going to therapy. One was between the ages of five and nine, and then I stopped going for a while and had to go again between the ages of eleven and fourteen

---

7 In psychology and sociology, masking refers to people camouflaging their personality or natural behavior to fit what is expected of them, to show the ideal image on social media, or even to prevent abuse or harassment.

because I still had difficulty communicating. My mother helped me differentiate things, and my father was also very present; he helped a lot with my directness or taking things literally; he helped me differentiate between reality, jokes, and lies. My father gave me the option of working in a foundation called "Sendero de Chile," where I learned different types of jobs, working with the land..., doing surveys..., and that's where I met my first girlfriend with whom I have been for 10 years, 10 months, and six days. She has supported me a lot, and I have supported her, too; we listen to each other and support each other in difficult times. We've traveled together here in Chile."

—"What message would you send to people with autism and families of people with autism?"

—"The first thing is that the earlier they are diagnosed, the better because then they will be able to receive the right therapies to progress. Many of us have anxiety disorders, depression, so it's important to tackle things early. I would also like to recommend that they look up a lot of information about how broad the autism spectrum is. There are different degrees; there are autistics who require therapy throughout their entire lives, and there are some who don't need much. We are fighting for the entire autistic community to have the same rights; we all have the right not to be discriminated against. I would like you to help and support us in this fight. I also want to tell you that some autistic people feel more identified with the infinity symbol with the rainbow colors, not with the piece of the puzzle because that tries to show how we are an incomplete piece or that we should fit into something, and we don't like to be seen that way, because we are not like that. And finally, I think it's very important to listen to the voices of autistic adults. Talk about us, but with us."

—"We associate autism almost always with involuntary movements or stimming. Do you have it? And what do you feel when you do them?"

—"Yes, I have it. One of the reasons we have these involuntary movements is that we need to self-regulate from tensions, noises, intolerance, frustrations, and having a lot of anger stored. I tend to do these involuntary flapping movements because that's how I self-regulate, and here, there is an issue of great concern: what happens if an autistic person starts flapping in a supermarket? People who don't know about autism are going to get scared, they're going to laugh, and probably the family of the autistic child will try to avoid taking this child along for fear that it starts flapping. I think it's essential to validate those involuntary movements and, of course, educate the population, explaining and understanding that if it's an autistic girl or boy and is self-regulating, you have to let it happen.   So, don't suppress *stimming* or stereotypies."

—"What skills do you think make you most special?"

—"Autistic people usually have some passion. We can spend all day looking at animals or numbers, literature or dinosaurs or planets, and we get very passionate about a subject, and we can talk about the same thing for a long time. When I was a kid, I talked all the time about sizes and things like that. We can be very smart in some areas. There are some autistics who have more problems, some cognitive, in some areas and many skills in others, so that varies a lot, but for example, in my case, I am very good with random dates, and I have a knack for mental calculations."

CHAPTER XV

The Mountain and The Squirrel or The Fable by Ralph Waldo Emerson

The mountain and the squirrel
Had a quarrel,
And the former called the latter
"Little prig."
Bun replied,
"You are doubtless very big;
But all sorts of things and weather
Must be taken in together
To make up a year
And a sphere.
And I think it no disgrace
To occupy my place.
If I'm not so large as you,
You are not so small as I,
And not half so spry:
I'll not deny you make
A very pretty squirrel track.
Talents differ; all is well and wisely put;
If I cannot carry forests on my back,
Neither can you crack a nut."

'If I had known, I wouldn't have cried so much,' I often repeat this to myself when I look back and see myself in various stages of my life as a mom and then compare it to the great and remarkable progress that Lucía is making every day.

I cried a lot, yes, because of the uncertainty, because of the serious mistake I made comparing my daughter with other children her age, because of all the time I didn't hear her voice, because I didn't see her walk around the house with the will of her own feet, because of the fear of not understanding what was happening, because I didn't know if I was doing it right. Because of the desperation caused by the unknown, the loneliness that we can feel after this type of diagnosis, even if we have the best of companies by our side. I cried where no one saw me, with all my might, especially her first two years, I cried so much that I got tired of crying and one day I started to make peace with myself, and I understood that this was not just about how I felt, but how I wanted my daughter to feel.

If you want someone to be proud of you, you must be proud of you first, and I want Lucía to be very proud of me. That's why I began to fall in love with every good and not-so-good moment I lived with her, with my tears and the sadness that I sometimes felt. I began to accept, without resentment, the inescapable fact that this diagnosis, in addition to being real, was necessary to give explanations and solutions to all the questions that I was not able to answer before. Why fight against what naturally already is? Why deny the obvious?

I decided not to focus on society's labels, and I began to fill in my gaps about autism or neurodivergence by reading, contrasting information, but, above all, listening and getting to know my daughter, her needs, and the different areas in which she had to work with her, not because of the imposition of a social norm, but because of her own desire for knowledge. Our children are the greatest teachers we will ever have, listening to them, understanding them, and not judging them should be one of our most important goals.

I would very much like that as a society, we learn to live with everything that is inside and outside the "norm", that we avoid many of the expectations that only generate frustration, and that competition is encouraged, yes, but among oneself, that each boy or girl is his or her own rival and goes beyond all his or her goals. That the "differences" are well received and do not mean a limitation for the acceptance of our children. And that, as in my favorite fable, everyone goes to their own job without judging the work or limitations of others.

If you ask me what I'm afraid of today, I will tell you that I'm no longer afraid of the diagnosis. Now, I'm afraid of what society can do with that diagnosis, of that which they don't want to accept or understand regarding certain behaviors, of the lack of patience. That's why I also wrote this book: to make visible all the small and big astronauts out there who are trying to understand our world from their innocent bubble.

Lucía continues to grow in size and in human greatness. She is wonderful, and she continues to surprise me all the time. I cannot imagine any other path as a mother than the one I am with by her side. I always say it: if fairy godmothers existed and gave me the possibility to grant me a wish, it would always be to have exactly the same daughter and go through the same process again;

I am the mother I am because I am the mother of Lucía Mia Valdés Valdés.

DAUGHTER

May your eyes continue to show me your soul.

May your hands draw each vowel in the air for a long time.

May your voice continue to create songs.

May You be proud of Me.

Beloved Lucia,

Whether or not you will be able to do certain things

when you grow up,

only time and you will tell.

I'll be here, for as long as life gives me the strength to.

Hopefully I have a lot of it, so that I can help push you when you get tired, to hug you when you make it

And tell you how proud I am of you when you cannot do certain things.

Thank you for giving me a ticket to your planet and teaching me how to orbit it.

Thank you for giving me the opportunity of being your mom.

CONTACTS

Octavio Vasconcello-Cohen MD

(305) 200-3992

8224 Mills Drive

Miami Fl 33183

Dr Emme Corrales

First Choice Neurology: Emme Corrales-Reyes, MD

(954) 686-7057

14201 W Sunrise Blvd STE 207, Sunrise, FL 33323

Florida Kids Therapy Medley

Judith Diaz

(786) 865-4646

Floridakidstherapy.com

@Floridakidstherapymedley

NOW WHAT?

After the results, the real work of being a mother or father begins, if you have already received a diagnosis, now start your own book.

It would be wonderful to be able to enter the minds of our children with autism and understand exactly how they think, what they feel, how they see the world, so that we can help them more, but since it is not possible so far, use all your strength and all your love.

Remember

YOU ARE NOT ALONE!

ASTRONAUT

SONG TO LUCIA

This song is one of the most beautiful, tender, and sublime I have ever heard. Written in a very delicate way and with deep love by Alexis Valdés, Lucia's father, and dedicated to all mothers and fathers, but above all, and very especially, to our autistic children. I liked it so much when I heard it, I was so moved that I wanted to leave you the song in an unpublished way, as it was recorded in the living room of the house and with his heart in his mouth. I hope you like it,

CLAUDIA VALDES

ABOUT THE AUTHOR

Claudia Valdés (Havana, Cuba) At the age of 7 she made her film debut as the protagonist in *Far from Africa*. She then participated in children's programs for television until at the age of 13 she entered the ENA (National School of Art), where she studied for four years.

Among her film works are *Los Dioses Rotos,* Larga *distancia, Mañana, La edad de la peseta, The Tainted Touch, Chico y Rita* and more recently *Club de Jazz.* In the theater she has worked as a producer and actress in several plays, among which are the successful comedy *Officially Gay, by* Alexis Valdés, *and* Felices los cuentos, *by the same director, as well as* Los vecinos de arriba, by *Cesc gay,* 8 mujeres, *the musical* El Club de las divorciadas, *Baño de Luna, by Nilo Cruz, Hierro,* by Carlos Celdrán, among many others. This is his first book.

ABOUT THE TRANSLATOR:

Lidice Megla (she/ her) is a Cuban Canadian hyphened poet and literary translator with several published poetry collections. An international poetry contest winner and a 2024 nominee for the Women of Influence Nanaimo (WIN) in the Arts and Culture category, a nature lover, and a dedicated translator with a collection that ranges from art brut to poetry, fiction, and nonfiction. A full member of the Literary Translators Association of Canada and the Federation of Writers of British Columbia, where she lives, works, and learns.

Her books can be found at
https://www.amazon.com/stores/author/B07XVT6D K8

TABLE OF CONTENTS

Every book is a trip to the Moon of Letters

lunetraeditorial@gmail.com

January 2024

Tampa, Florida, USA

Made in the USA
Columbia, SC
18 February 2024

31756141R00085